Also by Courtney LeBlanc

Beautiful & Full of Monsters
Exquisite Bloody, Beating Heart
Her Whole Bright Life

HER DARK EVERYTHING

Courtney LeBlanc

Riot in Your Throat
publishing fierce, feminist poetry

Copyright © Courtney LeBlanc, 2025

No part of this book may be used or performed without written consent from the author, if living, except for critical articles or reviews.

LeBlanc, Courtney.
1st edition.
ISBN: 979-8-9889898-6-8

Cover Art: Florian Olivo (www.unsplash.com)
Cover Design: Kirsten Birst
Book Design: Shanna Compton
Author Photo: Tay Lauren Photography

Riot in Your Throat
Arlington, VA
www.riotinyourthroat.com

for Virginia, my anchor

*I want to be inside your
darkest everything.*
—Frida Kahlo

CONTENTS

I

15 All at Once
16 Naming the Moon
17 After the Attempt
18 I Have Always Known
19 Abecedarian for Wanting to Die
20 I Can't Stop
22 If I Don't Complete the Thought You Will Never
23 The Length
24 I'm Teaching a Workshop on Titles and Couldn't Come Up with a Better One for This Poem
25 I Take a Break at Work to Sit in the Courtyard and am Attacked by Insects
26 A Fight Might Be a Celebration
27 Mad Libs for After She Dies
28 Again, My Dogs Save Me
30 Duplex for When She Died
31 Another Poem for You
32 21 Ways to End a Poem or Leave Your Lover
34 When Asked to Write About Something Bad I Did
35 Antilamentation
36 Meditations on the Heart
37 I Always Paint My Nails Black
38 ▌Always ███████████

II

43 My Friend Tells Me She'll Never Write Another Poem
44 We Live in America, Here's How We Survive

45 Apocalypse Poem
47 Prayer for the Broken
49 To the Man at the Gym Who Tried to "Help" Me with My Form
50 Poem Where I Apologize for Being a Woman
51 Both Girls & Wolves Have Sharp Teeth
52 Wild Delight
54 Duplex for the Not-Quite-Forgotten Girl
55 Ketamine: A Love Poem
56 I Try to Write a Poem While My Best Friend Gets a Ketamine Infusion for Her Depression
57 Find the Honey
58 Happiness
60 Belly Dancing as Love Poem
61 21 Months Since My Best Friend Began Ketamine Infusions for Her Depression as Math Problem
62 What the Living Do
63 Hope Is the Thing with Feathers
64 It's My Best Friend's 47th Birthday
65 Ode to My Best Friend

69 Acknowledgments & Notes
70 Thanks
72 About the Author
73 About the Press

I

To die will be an awfully big adventure.
　　　　　—*Peter Pan* by J. M. Barrie

ALL AT ONCE
—after Clint Smith

Everyone is posting pictures with twinkling lights. A bomb is dropped and a child's scream needs no translation. A friend on the other side of the world walks into a river, no rocks sewn into the hem because none are needed. Ketamine flows through your best friend's brain and a new path is forged and she begins to follow it out of the darkness. You allow yourself another cookie and for once, don't feel guilty about it. It begins to snow in Boston and across the country, someone posts a video of downhill skiing in the mud. You sign up for yoga, a month of Sundays, even though you don't really like all the spiritual *my inner teacher sees and acknowledges your inner teacher* BS. Your sister signs a lease and you mail a care package to her new address. A conflict—or is it a full-fledged war? Is there a difference?—everyone predicted would be over in weeks passes the two-year mark. You spend $270 on groceries and your spouse still says there's nothing to eat in the house. You take a muscle relaxer most nights and worry you're taking it too often. An ex-lover sends a message and you leave it unread for days. You look at the calendar and realize the year is almost over. You write a list. You avoid the news. It snows where your mother lives but you don't call her. You write in your journal. You think about the next year, your new goals, the way you're beginning to forget the sound of your father's voice. The lights are twinkling but they block out the stars. Somewhere, a woman dies, a lungful of water and a dark heart. Somewhere, a baby swims through the birth canal, pushes into the light. You don't believe in reincarnation but what if? What if?

NAMING THE MOON

When she tells me she doesn't want
to live anymore, I write a poem
which feels like a cop-out—
how can a poem help? But
she's a poet too, so I think she might
understand, might like this fucked-
up tribute. I know it's not
my responsibility to save her, but
I remind her the same moon
looks down on us. We only have
one floating in our sky and we're
boring humans because it's just
named Moon—clearly the poets
were not consulted. So I ask her:
what would you name the moon?
*Death, darkness, the end of everything,
I want to die,* she says. Tears crowd
my eyes but I say, *I'd name it hope.
Wonder. I'd name it stay one more night.*

AFTER THE ATTEMPT

She's selling her things, posting
each part of her identity: the Pilates
reformer, the beaded ball gown
she wore for her author pictures,
the plants she kept alive even when
she wanted to die. She's angry someone
intervened, angry she woke up
in the hospital. I tell her I'm glad
she's still here and she says, *I'm not.*
When I ask her to come to the workshop
I'm teaching in a month she says, *I hope
to be dead by then.* I don't know how
to respond so I tell her, *I love you.
I'm grateful you're here. The world is better
with you in it.* She leaves the message unread.

I HAVE ALWAYS KNOWN

Most of us discover we are the antagonist
long after the epilogue. But I have always
known the truth: I am disaster. I am wild-
fire. I am squall that swallows sailors
and mermaids alike. I am untamed
bronco refusing to be broken.
I am devastation. I am desire.
I am the very thing you crave.

ABECEDARIAN FOR WANTING TO DIE

After the last failed attempt the blackness
blossomed, spread through every neuron,
crept like ivy into every synapse,
dove deep into her heart,
entangled itself in the deep
fissures of her mind until she was
guided down a singular path:
how to successfully die.
I don't know exactly how she did it,
just that she finally did, and
knowing the details doesn't change the truth: she no
longer lives. I've accepted this,
mostly—I couldn't
nudge her brain back into the light.
Oh how I tried, sent words of love, tried to
prop her up in the
rickety
scaffolding of my own heart,
tried to keep her head above the darkness that constantly pulled her
under. But my
various attempts would never be enough, she
wanted to die. To follow the map that led to
X: the place she no longer existed, the
yellow brick road leading to the
zenith of her life.

I CAN'T STOP
—*after Jeannine Hall Gailey*

being a person who imagines
every footfall behind me on a trail
is a serial rapist. Or being nervous
in a dark parking lot. Or burying
my nose in the lilacs that bloom
along my back fence. I worry
the bees are dying, the polar bears
are starving, the ice caps are
melting. Also, I always stop
and photograph fiddleheads,
their green unfurling reminds
me of rebirth. And the wineberries
that grow wild, the sun-warmed
fruit crushed between my teeth.
I can't stop comparing the defense
budget to the education budget.
I watch the Super Bowl and think
of brains bounced against bone. I eat
a brownie and think of my thighs
thickening. But also, I turn
my face to the sun and don't think
about it burning or the Earth's
rotation slowing or skin cancer.
I just feel the warm on my skin.
I'd rather tell you about the first
tomato that has sprouted in my
small garden, of the net I use
to keep those damn squirrels
away. I wonder if marriages
are always this hard and if my dog

will shit on the carpet again today.
But also, I can't stop smiling
at every rainbow as they kaleidoscope
across the sky. Today I wonder
if I'll be able to deliver my father's
eulogy without crying and if I should
wear waterproof mascara. I can't
stop finding poems in every
heartache. But I'd rather tell you
about my nonstop love for a
Skillcraft permanent fine point
pen, the way the ink flows on
the paper, the way it brings life
to the words I write. I can't stop
thinking about the mistake I made
3 years, 8 months, 6 days, and 12 hours
ago. But let me tell you of my dog's
nose pressed against my hand, the weight
of my husband's arm dropped over
my hip, of that first sip of coffee as the sun
rises and banishes the night.

IF I DON'T COMPLETE THE THOUGHT YOU WILL NEVER
—after Frances Klein, after Amy Miller

the river rushes by, without a body

the pills sit on your tongue, unswallowed

the potted plants continue greening
on your windowsill instead of

your car drives past the turnout, doesn't

the letters do not burst from your mailbox,
waiting for

the emails don't go unread

I don't google your name ten times a day
for two weeks hoping

THE LENGTH

The length between
typing your name and hitting
enter is a lifetime. The length
between the page loading
and my eyes dropping
to the first result is a million
breaths. The length between
registering the words *body*
and *identified* is a millennium.
The length between a sea filling
my eyes and the tides rushing
down my cheeks is a heartbeat.
The length between already knowing
you're gone and having the proof glare
at me is an eyelash lifted softly
from my cheek, the breath held
inside my lungs, knowing my wish
can never come true.

I'M TEACHING A WORKSHOP ON TITLES AND COULDN'T COME UP WITH A BETTER ONE FOR THIS POEM

You're the queen of titles, I tell her
ghost. In my memories she's always
wearing a ball gown: the deep
blue velvet one with the cape
that looked like the night sky,
each silver strand woven into
a constellation against the dark
fabric. Or the emerald green
one with sleeves as delicate
as spiderwebs. Or the blood-
red dress with the black lace
overlay that made her look
like a vampire queen. *Were you
wearing a dress when you swallowed
the pills? When you went into the water?*
I ask her ghost. She doesn't
answer, just arches a perfect
brow. She'll always live like this
in my memory: gowned
and glorious, gorgeous in her
sadness, the princess of agony,
the queen of despair and titles
that opened into a brittle beauty.

I TAKE A BREAK AT WORK TO SIT IN THE COURTYARD AND AM ATTACKED BY INSECTS

I came here to think of you, to avoid
crying in my office or in the bathroom.
To tip my head back and let the sun
warm my face. Instead gnats swarm me
and I spend ten minutes swatting them
away, barely thinking of you. They haven't
found your body yet but I know you're dead.
You gave me the exact date, told me, *I have to
move out in six weeks and five days and so I plan
to be dead before then.* I pulled out a calendar,
counted the days. But when that Thursday
arrived I forgot to message you, forgot
to remind you of my love. I'm not dumb
enough to think I could have saved you
but my heart is struggling to believe anything.
I smash a bug against my skin, wipe away
the guts—everything dies in the end.
Me, you, these gnats. I think of how brave
you must have been in those moments,
to finally give in to what you'd wanted
for so many years. To finally find the dark
embrace of death and call it home.

A FIGHT MIGHT BE A CELEBRATION

*"The tango is a direct expression of something
that poets have often tried to state in words:
the belief that a fight might be a celebration."*
—Jorge Luis Borges

They still haven't found your body, but
I've learned the Manawatū River leads
to the ocean, the water you (likely) walked
into could have, eventually, carried you
to the sea. Maybe that's not so bad, to be held
in the water's embrace, to move with the flow
of the current. You knew how to tango,
and in the last two weeks of your life
you posted videos of gliding across
a floor, your body still agile. Maybe
it felt like dancing, trusting the river
to be your partner, to move you
where you needed to go.

MAD LIBS FOR AFTER SHE DIES

You're _____ (verb ending in -ing) when you learn the news: she's dead. You feel _____ (emotion) and _____ (emotion). You _____ (verb), as if this could change the truth. The _____ (type of bird, plural) don't fall from the sky, the _____ (animal, plural) don't retreat into caves, the _____ (body of water) doesn't flow backwards, doesn't dry up, doesn't stop being wet. She was full of _____ (emotion), her poems full of _____ (noun, plural). You thought she'd always _____ (action verb), always exist. She didn't say goodbye, instead she just _____ (past tense verb).

AGAIN, MY DOGS SAVE ME

I once hiked six miles in a hot
pink tutu. The water cupped
from the stream was cool in my
hands, the tulle of the tutu
stuck to my sweat-slick
legs. The most normal thing
that day: my dogs, blissfully
unaware of the fracture gnawing
at my heart. You'd been declared
dead, your body not yet found,
but I knew the declaration to be
true. I plucked wineberries from
the bushes that bloomed
along the trail, my juice-stained
fingers matching my skirt. I didn't try
to stop the tears, just let them fall
onto the berries. My dogs pulled
me forward, refusing to let me
wet the bushes. I wore this
skirt because you, my declared-
dead friend, loved elaborate
gowns, loved velvet and tulle
and silver thread spiderwebbed
through soft fabric. You loved
drama and glamour and so
I lipsticked my mouth, pulled
on the only skirt that made sense,
and went into the woods to cry.
I saw no other humans that day
on the trail and the woodland

creatures stayed away too—
fairies and foxes alike, both
banished by my tears. Maybe
the trees were giving me space
to grieve, maybe the stream
was trying to carry away
my sadness, maybe nature
saw how fucking absurd
I looked—snot-streaked face,
fuchsia tulle stuck to my skin,
my mouth grinning through
my grief, and my dogs pulling
me forward. Always forward.

DUPLEX FOR WHEN SHE DIED

I knew the day she was going to die, forgot to call,
      wrapped up in my own life as hers slipped away.

She slipped into the water, her life floated away,
      lungs filled, her midnight-blue ballgown floated around her.

She loved dramatic gowns: blaze-red, indigo with sequins: stars against a midnight sky.
      I always picture her this way, as if she never wore anything else.

She always wore her sadness, couldn't picture her life without it.
      When she went into the water, she carried it with her.

The water carried away her sadness, finally wrenched it from her.
      I'll never forget her, will always call her up in my memory.

ANOTHER POEM FOR YOU

The grief sits heavy on my heart, a boulder
I'll carry always, I'll worry it smooth until it fits

perfectly, an outer shell that will do nothing
to protect me. I'm not mad you're dead but

I hate it. You honored your grief the only way
you could when you walked into that river,

let the water drift between your fingers,
your sequined skirt swirling around you like

iridescent seaweed. Would you be glad
to know I've written a poem for you every

damn day this week? Or would you laugh
and say, *Oh Courtney, I'm not worth*

writing about. How wrong you'd be.

21 WAYS TO END A POEM OR LEAVE YOUR LOVER

1. Board the plane. Don't look back at the departure gate, just walk down the jetway, store your carry-on and find your seat.
2. Make it big and dramatic. Hire a sky writer. Send a dozen roses with the heads cut off. Tattoo his name with a line drawn straight through it.
3. Stop talking to him. No explanation, no goodbye, no *Dear John* note scrawled in ink. Just silence.
4. Be cliché. Lipstick a message in your favorite color across the mirror. Let your final kiss be on glass instead of her lips.
5. Speak only in metaphor. Compare your lover to the wildfires that rage through forests, destroying everything in their path until they run out of oxygen or kindling. You are the kindling. She is the fire. And also the oxygen.
7. Tell her, *I don't love you*, even if you do.
7. Cut his image from every picture, slice them into confetti and the next time you want to call him, throw it into the air. Vacuum the floors instead of picking up your phone.
8. Listen to your favorite Ani DiFranco songs. Sing them loudly with the windows down and the volume up.
9. Forbid anyone to say his name. Strike it from your vocabulary, delete him from your lexicon.
10. Imagine she's stuck on an island and you'll never see her again. Imagine her shipwrecked. Imagine her as a shipwreck, sunk in the blue-green depths, home only to barnacles and seaweed.
11. Do it just before midnight on New Year's Eve. Kiss a stranger instead.
12. Show up at his doorstep at 2am with a bottle of champagne. Fuck him until the sun starts to peak from behind the buildings. Drink the champagne with burned toast. Drop the bottle in the recycling when you leave.
13. Gather everything he ever gave you and burn it in the backyard. Dance naked around the flames. When the fire department shows up, kiss every firefighter in thanks.

14. Move into a new apartment, one with no memories of her—where she pressed you against a wall, where she fucked you in the sun-drenched living room. Leave no forwarding address.
15. Take a trip by yourself. Explore a country where you don't speak the language. Kiss a stranger who can't pronounce your name.
16. Adopt the dog she never wanted. Give it her middle name. Let it sleep in the bed beside you.
17. Go see his favorite band without him. If you can, fuck the lead singer. If you can't, settle for the drummer. Post pictures with the band on social media. Tag him.
18. Kiss him like someone who has learned a foreign language but only the present tense and only 2nd person: only now, only you.
19. Break up with him on his birthday. Bake him a cake and in tiny candies spell out across the top: *Happy Birthday, it's over!*
20. Hold her hand and tell her you just can't anymore. Cry as both your hearts break.
21. Like this.

WHEN ASKED TO WRITE ABOUT SOMETHING BAD I DID
—*after Brett Elizabeth Jenkins*

I hand over my marriage certificate, the lace garter that hugged
my thigh the day I said *I do,* the racy emails sent to a man who didn't
share my last name. I pull out my passport, turn to the page stamped
with Paris and find the receipt for the expensive lingerie I bought
with another in mind, the satin bows and braiding pushing my tits up
high enough for even God to appreciate them. I hand over my driver's
license because at 22 I drove drunk and I'm still shocked I didn't end
up in a ditch. I forgot to call her the day she went into the river and met
her end. I don't know my older sister's birthday—August, yes, but what
year? I have a vague memory of skinny-dipping with someone's boyfriend
but both names and faces have been erased from my memory. I could
arrange each regret by color, by code, by how heavy they hang in my heart.
I have regrets I could alphabetize. I will make more; I can promise you that.

ANTILAMENTATION
—after Dorianne Laux

Regret nothing, not the night you stayed
awake till 3am reading even though your
alarm was set for 5am because you had
to know whodunit. Those dark circles
can hide behind concealer and an extra
cup of coffee—the plot twist at the end
was worth it. Not the extra glasses of wine
or the salty cheese that melted on your tongue,
the conversation with friends that carried you
through four bottles and probably 1,000 calories.
Don't regret the movie you watched on the 14-hour
flight, the one that made you ugly cry and caused
your seatmate to hand you a tissue and pat
your arm, as if he too understood the heartbreak
Bradley Cooper can induce. Don't regret the time
spent traveling his body with your hands, the
salt water smell that always takes you back
to the island of his love. Don't dwell
on the tattoo you got on your 18th birthday,
even if they didn't call them tramp
stamps yet. Don't worry, just sit with
your journal and a pen and the early
morning sky and write and write and write.

MEDITATIONS ON THE HEART
—after Cameron Awkward-Rich

I wake up and it breaks my heart.
I walk my dogs before the sun begins
to pink the sky and it breaks my heart.
I skim the headlines because I can't
even bear reading the news: break-
break-break. My best friend texts
about her own sad heart and I pull
the seams of mine together—we can't
both be broken. I strip naked,
the salty sweat of my workout the only
thing I wear as I step onto the scale—
every day, every tenth of a pound,
the difference: the number either
breaks or lifts my heart. I scratch
my dogs' bellies, curl up with them
on the couch and my heart stitches
itself back together again. I look
at the calendar, my dead father's
birthday is soon. The grief still
breaks my heart. I'm trying to learn
to wholly love myself, I promise.
I trying to learn to swim with grief
instead of letting it drown me,
I promise. Hand on my heart.
Hand on my stupid heart.

I ALWAYS PAINT MY NAILS BLACK

& sometimes my husband teases me & says, *Black again? They make other colors, right?* & of course they do but I love black nails & every time they're freshly painted I feel sexy as fuck & so I'm probably not going to get any other color & in art, black is the presence of all colors & my friend Paula always painted her nails dark too & she's dead now & I knew the day she was going to do it, the exact date, I knew it & I forgot to call & I forgot to text & I know I couldn't have saved her & I hope the water she walked into held her & I hope the pills she swallowed gentled her journey & I go whole days without thinking of her & then I feel like shit but I know she'd want me to forget & I do think of her whenever I read a sexy poem because she wrote such damn good sexy poems & I think she'd like that I think of her then & the first person who asked me how I wanted to be touched painted his pinkie nails black each weekend & removed it each Monday morning & I can still see his face & I still remember his hands on my body & it was the first time I wasn't afraid of my body or its pleasure & that was the same summer "Push" by Matchbox Twenty was playing nonstop on the radio & the lead singer painted his nails black & it was the first time I'd seen nail polish on a guy & I liked it & I was eighteen & I'd just moved into my first basement apartment & I was fucking Brit, the boy with the black-painted pinkies & I was so young & so free & I rarely painted my nails then & now I'm never without polish & my best friend loves pedicures & she always gets the same color too, a shade of red called "I'm not really a waitress" & she tried to die several times & she's still here & I'm so fucking grateful & she finally found a treatment to rewire her brain & I wish Paula had found peace & was still here & still writing sexy poems & still painting her nails dark. But she's not. So I am.

ALWAYS

& sometimes   & every time
                                    & I'm probably not
                                                    & my friend Paula
always   & she's dead now
                                        & I forgot   & I forgot
& I know I couldn't   & I hope
                                                          & I go whole days
without   & then I feel like   I   want   to
forget & I do
                                                                          &
the first person   I wanted to   touch
            each weekend &   each   morning & I can still
              & I still remember   & it was the first time I
wasn't afraid of   pleasure & that   same summer
                              was   nonstop
                          & it was the first time   &
I liked it & I was eighteen
& I was fucking   the boy   & I was so
young & so free   & now I'm never without
          & my best friend loves
                                              & she tried to die several times
& she's still here & I'm so fucking grateful & she finally
                        & I wish Paula   peace & was still here & still
                                                      she's not.

II

Hope is the thing with feathers.
—Emily Dickinson

MY FRIEND TELLS ME SHE'LL NEVER WRITE ANOTHER POEM

and I immediately write one about her / because once we sat
in a hotel lobby with a bottle of champagne between us, passing

it back and forth by the neck, taking small sips because gulping
champagne bubbles up your nose / because she gave me a lipstick

called *intrigue* and every time I roll it over my lips I think of her
/ because she adopts dogs the way I buy books / because she can

bake bread and I always kill the yeast / because we both curse
in our poems and in our lives and when I first met her I knew

she was a forever friend / because she's read nearly every damn
poem I've written in the past five years / because I love her laugh

and her quiet poems / because this isn't the end of our friendship but
change is scary and even at 44 years old sometimes

it's hard to say that / because maybe she'll read this and write
her own poem / or maybe she won't / or maybe in three years

she'll fill an entire journal in a month because those goddamn words
have to get out / but even if she doesn't, I'll still be here / because

WE LIVE IN AMERICA, HERE'S HOW WE SURVIVE

We get up each morning, walk
our dogs, brew our coffee and maybe
take a minute to stare out into the brightening
sky, a moment of refuge before we read
the news, scroll through our feed, before
we pull on running shoes to beat the pavement
and try to leave our troubles on the road,
then rush to the first meeting of our day.
We sign petitions and donate money and go
door-to-door, campaigning. We watch the news
on mute, crying—sometimes tears of joy,
usually not. We put on lipstick even if it's hidden
behind a mask. We text our friends and meet
in front of the Supreme Court in supportive
shoes and comfortable bras. We scream
and chant and hold the signs we thought
we no longer needed.

APOCALYPSE POEM

I keep thinking of the apocalypse
as a singular event: zombies rising
up to feast on flesh, a virus so vicious
90% of the world is dead in a year,
a tsunami swallowing the west coast,
an asteroid crashing into the soft
earth of the desert, a slow cloud
of grit choking out the sun
and our bones becoming fossils
some future generation digs up,
fascinated by the small rectangular
boxes clutched in our hands. Instead,
the apocalypse is already happening.
Each day someone walks into
a school with a gun in hand
and a backpack full of bullets
instead of books, it's an apocalypse.
Every time a cop pulls a trigger
while hands are lifted in the air
and we have another hashtag,
it's an apocalypse. Every time
dividing cells are protected instead
of women, our civilization dies
a little. There's not going to be
a *big one*, there won't be any
end-of-world parties with excess
cheese and chocolate and that
expensive bottle of champagne
you've been saving for a special
occasion—those are for movies

and books sold in airports.
In the apocalypse, that thing we're
swimming through now, fighting
to keep our heads above water
unsafe to drink, it'll be softer.
It'll be the wearing down
of your empathy, your endurance,
your fight. It'll look like today
and yesterday and tomorrow.

PRAYER FOR THE BROKEN
   —after Mindee Nettifee

Be broken. Lie
down on the cold
ground, feel rocks
under your back. Listen
to the wind howl. Rage
with it, let it lift your scream
to the heavens. Sing
off-key. Change
the lyrics until they fit
like a hand-sewn dress.
Walk barefoot
into the river, feel
the water pull you forward,
let it wash you clean
of every regret
you hide in your heart.
Swim to the other side
and when you get to that
bank, sink your feet into
the mud, feel it squish
between your toes.
Let the words of gratitude
build like a tidal wave
inside you, let it wash
over you. Tell the mud
and the trees and the river
and the wind, *thank you.*
Yell it until your voice gravels.
Breathe. Know there is enough
air for your lungs. Taste

how sweet it is, how your chest
expands with it, how your blood
sings in response. Spread
your arms wide, feel the sun
kiss your face and know it will
come again tomorrow and
tomorrow and tomorrow
again.

TO THE MAN AT THE GYM WHO TRIED TO "HELP" ME WITH MY FORM

I see you, your back curved like
a comma as you choose a weight
too heavy. My own back straight
as the line I walk every time I'm
in the gym: don't linger too long
at the weight bench or some burly
fellow will surely think I need his help.
Don't flex in the mirror because I'm just
inviting a man to stand beside me,
flexing in return as he tries to catch
my eye. Earbuds in but nothing
playing—just the dull ache of
awareness, my mind on my reps
and the fool in the tight tank top
who keeps trying to spot me. We
women watch each other's backs,
keep the creeps from crowding.
After an hour I wipe down
the equipment, leave with my back
as straight as the stick up my ass—
according to the man who didn't
get my number, despite his ability
to bench twice my body weight,
despite his thick hands squeezing
my shoulder in unearned camaraderie.
Tomorrow I'll return, ready
to lift or run or urge my body
to do a few more push-ups. Tomorrow
I'll return, invisible armor in place,
a weight no man has ever had to lift.

POEM WHERE I APOLOGIZE FOR BEING A WOMAN

Of course it's my fault, I obviously don't know
how to take a joke. And yes, you're right,
it was a compliment and what woman wouldn't
want her body commented on by a stranger
passing on the street? Yes, I wore this
dress/these shorts/this ruffled tank top
for your viewing pleasure, not because I feel
confident/comfortable/cute in it. Of course
when you watched that woman walking away
you were thinking about her accomplishments,
her goals, and not the swish of her hips, the sway
of her ass. I'm sure the man that got the promotion
I interviewed for is highly qualified and uniquely
positioned to lead the office I've been a part of
for 6 years. And yes, I do know how to do a chest
press and lat pulldowns but thank you for your offer
to assist me. Oh yes, it is a bit dramatic, all this #MeToo
stuff, I mean, Bill Cosby went to jail for a little while
and eventually Harvey Weinstein was punished. Never
mind it took years and left dozens of destroyed women
in their wake. And you're right, if we aren't careful
it'll swing the other way and women will be the majority—
lawyers and doctors and dentists—and we wouldn't want
that. True, we have our first female Vice President and she's
a woman of color at that, we should be happy, that really
is more than we could have hoped for. But maybe, maybe
fuck apologizing. Maybe fuck saying *I'm sorry* when I'm
really not, when I've done nothing wrong, when I have nothing
to apologize for.

BOTH GIRLS & WOLVES HAVE SHARP TEETH

When I was thirteen the brackets
went on, the metal strung back
and forth, up and down, a drunk
weaving between each tooth.
I ran my tongue along the sharp
edges, the inside of my lips torn
and ragged, the tender flesh
catching on the new apparatus.
The thick retainer kept my top
teeth from crashing down
onto the shark row of my
bottom jaw, months of slowly
adjusting my overbite. Rubber
bands and headgear, four teeth
pulled from the soft of my gums—
the roots thick and gnarled, tiny
trees in my mouth. Three and a half
years later, the last silver bracket
removed, the glue polished off,
the surface smoothed. The last
step: the subtle rounding of my
canines, the fangs I'd had my whole
life, shaped into something less
fierce, less feral. Something softer,
to pull my smile into the feminine
ideal, further from the wolves
that ran wild in my mouth.

WILD DELIGHT

When I was 17 I climbed onto the backs
of strangers' motorcycles. Didn't matter
who they were, I didn't care, I just wanted
to go fast, to feel the wind rush through
my thick hair like a tornado. We never
wore helmets, never saw most of them
again, maybe never even exchanged
names. I wrapped my arms around their
torsos, pressed my thighs against
their thighs and whispered, *Go faster,*
at stoplights, my hot breath turning to screech
of stupid delight when the light changed
and they dropped the bike into gear
and we shot into the night, sweat
and adrenaline and lust seeping
from our skin. Now, in my forties, I won't
ride a bicycle without a helmet, haven't
been on the back of a motorcycle
in years. I'm glad I did it then, lived
so fearlessly. I'm glad I felt the rush
of power between my legs, felt those
boy's hands reach back and touch
my calf, my thigh, felt the surge
of freedom and foolishness when
I was too young to know the risk,
too young to weigh the odds and decide
they weren't in my favor. I'll never
do it again, live like that. But damn,
those hot summer nights on the back
of a bike, my hair so wind-tangled

it would take my friend two hours to pick
it slowly free, those nights I was a reckless
banshee, a wild delight, a girl who took
life into her hands and demanded more.

DUPLEX FOR THE NOT-QUITE-FORGOTTEN GIRL

We were seventeen, bright-eyed and fresh-skinned.
I didn't yet understand the feelings blooming in my heart.

My heart bloomed like a flower—pink and full when
you smiled shyly at me.

Your smile wasn't coy, you were too shy for that.
We sat side by side on the couch, almost touching.

Our fingers almost touched, our thighs so close on the couch.
You looked like Winona Ryder—pixied and petite.

When I pixie my hair, it's equally of you and Winona Ryder.
Years later I will hunt through my memories for your name.

I can't remember your name, my teenage memories dull with age.
I wish I'd had the courage to kiss you then.

I wish I'd kissed you that night on the couch
but I was seventeen, uncertain of what my bright life could bring.

KETAMINE: A LOVE POEM

I watch as the ditch of her elbow is swabbed,
the needle gentled into her arm, the fog-gray
blanket placed over her lap, the eye mask pulled
down, music piped in as the liquid flows into her veins.

CAN PRODUCE FEELINGS OF UNREALITY:
But her reality is bleak—filled only with the desire
to die. So yes, please, let's have the unreality.

SENSORY DISTORTIONS OFTEN REPORTED:
Thank goodness. Let's bring in a grass so green she
cannot imagine not walking barefoot across it,
let's hope she smells campfire mingling in her hair,
hears the laughter of her son, feels the urgent
caress of her lover.

MAY CAUSE EUPHORIA: What a grand idea!
Let's hope this happens because she married
her sadness—a teen bride unable to divorce
the dread. She's carried around that deadbeat
for nearly thirty years.

This is a love letter to ketamine, to the drug
that swam through my best friend's veins
and brought her back to me. This is a love
letter to her smile, no longer a placeholder.
This is a love letter to her brain that followed
ketamine's path to the promise of a different
future. This is a love letter to her heart,
which still beats in her chest, to her goddamn
heart—steady and strong and determined to stay.

I TRY TO WRITE A POEM WHILE MY BEST FRIEND GETS A KETAMINE INFUSION FOR HER DEPRESSION

Like the Mariana Trench, I imagine a hole
darker and deeper than I've ever seen
in real life. It's not filled with spiders
or lizards or cobwebs or spindly roots—
it's just black and endless. This is my best
friend's depression, a hole so fathomless
she told her therapist she can do it
for five more years. *It* being life—living
and breathing and existing. So they're trying
something new, a drug that isn't fully
understood dancing with a brain that isn't
fully understood. She cries a little and says
bits of nonsense as the clear liquid waltzes
down the tube and into her vein. I sit
in the room with her, watching and waiting
for the drug to work its magic, to make
the right connections, to stop the dark
sadness from winning.

FIND THE HONEY

I'm trying to write about joy, trying
to find honey in the words, trying
to lick it from my fingertips and let
it be enough. It's hard when my belly
craves the dark sharpness of grief,
the hard edges of heartache. I'm looking
for the soft edges I can rub against
the inside of my wrist, caress the gentle
pink parts of me. I want to remember
the rainbows that grace the sky after
the storm but I only desire the rage
of thunder and lightning and a rain
so heavy you have to pull over to keep
from crashing. Maybe I can have both,
hold the moon in one hand and the sun
in the other. Maybe I can love you
and still let you go.

HAPPINESS
—after Jane Kenyon and with a borrowed line

There's just no accounting for happiness,
the way it finds you crouching in the dark
of your closet, hiding from the smallest
sliver of light. Because how can you forget
the way your dog launches toward you
each day, her need to say *good morning*
with every inch of her 50-pound body.
And how the sun begins to peek over
the rooftops as you walk, the days just
beginning to edge into autumn. Your
husband, still half asleep as he starts
the espresso machine, yawning as it
rumbles to life. How he makes your
latte first, always. And the books
stacked on your bedside table
and your hold list at the library
and all the books you've yet
to discover. Happiness worms
its way in, the smile your face can't
contain when you see the man
dancing down the street, his head
tilted back and arms wide, music
streaming into his ears and forcing
his body to move. The Thai food
delivered the night you're too tired
to cook, the smile when you tip in
cash, the smell of chili sauce filling
your nose. And when a new episode
of your favorite show drops and you
curl up on the couch, one dog snuggled

behind your legs, the other draped
across your lap—this is when
happiness finds you.

BELLY DANCING AS LOVE POEM

Years ago we took a belly dancing class together which was basically us just laughing at one another as we attempted to mimic our teacher's fluid hips, swinging side to side like liquid sex, laughing when the teacher told me I *didn't have enough belly* and you *didn't have enough butt* and we agreed but that didn't stop us from trying, our hips wrapped with gemstone colored scarves, mine green and yours fuchsia, gold bells tinkling softly, the perfect accompaniment to our laughter and clunky movements, our hips not so much sashaying as jerking from side to side, each shift of our bodies timed to our raucous laughter and I never danced for a lover, never wore that emerald scarf outside of class, never dared display my not-as-sexy-as-I-imagined moves to another—only you witnessed me, arms above my head, eyes closed as I moved my body to the same music you heard and when I opened my eyes I saw you'd done the same: eyes closed, arms up in abandon and I knew, in that moment, I'd never love anyone as much as I loved you.

21 MONTHS SINCE MY BEST FRIEND BEGAN KETAMINE INFUSIONS FOR HER DEPRESSION AS MATH PROBLEM
—*after Julia Kolchinsky*

21 months = ~630 days = the amount of time she hasn't wanted to die < 24.3 years we've known each other < 30 years which is how long she's wanted to die = her entire adult life – how she feels post-ketamine treatment × my love for her × driving her to appointments – the tears I cried in the waiting room + her saying, *before treatment I wanted to die every day* (averaging 2 on a scale of 1–10, 1 being you are planning to die by suicide, 10 being you're as happy as imaginable) + after treatment she's at a 7–8 = my 8-ounce heart lifting = she's going to stay = I can tuck my fear into a back closet in my 3-pound brain × this year I know 2 women who have died by suicide + the year isn't over × I'm still scared she'll decide to die × what if my love isn't enough × what if my love isn't enough × what if my love isn't enough = I wouldn't be able to breathe without her + I'm still afraid I'll lose her = she is my anchor = I am her anchor, tethering her to this life

WHAT THE LIVING DO
   —after Marie Howe

Paula, the weather has turned cold and I do not like it.
I've pulled out my hat and gloves, moved my wool
coat to the front of the closet and now it takes time
to dress before I can take the dogs out, their impatience
growing as I wind my scarf around my neck, pull
my hat down over my ears. The days are shrinking
shorter, we have twenty-one more days until the world
reverses itself and the light starts to lengthen. By winter
solstice you'll be gone six months, never again
to experience winter or summer or rain or shine.
Sometimes I go all day without thinking of you
and then I see a sequined shirt in my closet and think
of your dazzling gowns of velvet and tulle,
your quiet glamour. Your poems of sadness and sex.
This is what the living do: we walk our dogs
in the darkness. We layer against the cold
and against the hurt. We write poems
to dead friends to keep them alive.

HOPE IS THE THING WITH FEATHERS

A year ago my best friend wanted
to die, wanted to give in to the dark
craving that knocked at her door
for thirty years. Instead, she took
a chance on a new treatment
and today hope flutters inside
her chest, wings caressing her,
the dark fading from her heart.
I have always worried I will lose
her, worried one day she'll open
the door and let the darkness
saunter in, take her. I walk
my dogs each morning
in birdsong—spring is coming.
I let it flutter against my ribs,
I let it carry me through the day.

IT'S MY BEST FRIEND'S 47TH BIRTHDAY

and we do nothing. I'm wearing octopus-
print leggings and a sweater long enough to cover
my middle-aged butt. She's in old jeans and a Snoopy
sweatshirt, our faces free of makeup, hair swept
back in messy buns. We eat the lunch she made
(tempeh salad on toast), then the madeleines
I baked the day before. We fill champagne flutes
with the bubbly water we now both substitute
and raise our glasses high. We toast another year
just like this.

ODE TO MY BEST FRIEND

Long ago you swallowed the keys to the diary
of my heart, my secrets forever safe inside you.

Holder of my hand through marriages and divorce,
my life pledged to you before I ever took another.

Cheap pink wine drunk from straws, paired with Nacho
Cheese Doritos. Dancing until the lights came on

and the sweat crusted our skin. Surgeries and starving.
Madeleines and marathons. Recovery and replaying the last

message. Birth and babies. Ketamine infusions and calorie
counting. Massages and mass shootings. Lockdowns and breakdowns.

Twenty-five years of postcards and poems.
Twenty-five years of anchoring each other in this world.

ACKNOWLEDGMENTS & NOTES

The poet kindly thanks the following journals which first gave her poems a home, sometimes in earlier forms:
    Elysium Review: "My Friend Tells Me She'll Never Write Another Poem"
    Grist: "Both Girls & Wolves Have Sharp Teeth"
    Rogue Agent: "Belly Dancing as Love Poem"
    The Ilanot Review: "I Always Paint My Nails Black"
    Westchester Review: "After the Attempt"

"I Have Always Known" was included in the Moving Words Poetry Program and was displayed on the Arlington Transit (ART) buses in 2023

"Mad Libs for After She Dies" was inspired by "Mad Libs for When You're Not Writing" by Kelli Russell Agodon and Melissa Studdard

"21 Ways to End a Poem or Leave Your Lover" borrows its title from a blog post by Alina Stefanescer. Much of #18 in the list is borrowed from the novel "Less" by Andrew Sean Greer

"Ketamine: A Love Poem" was inspired by "Sertraline: A Prescription Zuihitsu" by Cynthia Manick

"Happiness" borrows its title and the first line, "There's just no accounting for happiness . . ." from "Happiness" by Jane Kenyon

"Meditations on the Heart" was inspired by "Meditations in an Emergency" by Cameron Awkward-Rich and borrows the first and last lines of that poem.

"Hope Is the Thing with Feathers" is a nod to Emily Dickinson's poem "'Hope' is the thing with feathers"

THANKS

First and foremost, thank you to my best friend, my soulmate, the keeper of my secrets, the holder of my hand, the anchor that keeps me grounded—thank you Virginia. The universe knew what it was doing when it brought us together. You are my bestest best friend and I cannot imagine life without you. Thank you for cheering me on, holding me up, and being the most amazing woman I know. Thank you for always fighting and thank you for staying. These past 26 years have been wonderful, I can't wait to see what the future holds for us.

Thank you to my husband, Jay, and my sister, Kirsten—you both support me and are excited for every new poetry project I undertake. Thank you for your unwavering support.

Thank you to the December Poets, the Emotional Historians, Community Building Art Works, and the Poetry Coven. Each of these writing groups inspired, nurtured, and made space for many of these poems. Thank you to the people who created these groups and to the people who participated in them. Thanks especially to Laura Passin and Melissa Fite Johnson—you have become such dear friends and I'm grateful for your friendship, your inspiration, and your poems.

Thank you to my feedback group: Amy Haddad, Ashley Steineger, and Caroline Earleywine—your feedback and poems make me a better writer.

To my dogs, Piper and Cricket. Dogs can't read but they deserve all the pets, love, and praise. Their giant hearts save me time and again.

Thank you to Kelli Russell Agodon, Joan Kwon Glass, and Bree Bailey for the kind and generous blurbs.

Thank you to Shanna Compton for the beautiful interior book design and to Kirsten Birst for the gorgeous cover design.

Many of the poems in this collection were inspired by my friend Paula Harris, who died by suicide in June 2023. Paula was an amazing poet who suffered chronic pain and severe depression. The world is less glamorous without her in it, but I am grateful she is no longer in pain. Paula from the future—you are missed.

Thank you to anyone who suffers from depression and continues to fight. Depression is a liar—you are wanted and needed and loved. I hope you stay.

ABOUT THE AUTHOR

Courtney LeBlanc is the author of the full-length collections *Her Dark Everything; Her Whole Bright Life* (winner of the Jack McCarthy Book Prize); *Exquisite Bloody, Beating Heart;* and *Beautiful & Full of Monsters*. She is the Arlington County Poet Laureate and the founder and editor-in-chief of *Riot in Your Throat,* an independent poetry press. She is also the founder of the Poetry Coven, a monthly generative workshop. She loves nail polish, tattoos, and a soy latte each morning. Find her online at www.courtneyleblanc.com.

ABOUT THE PRESS

Riot in Your Throat is an independent press that publishes fierce, feminist poetry.

Support independent authors, artists, and presses.

Visit us online:
www.riotinyourthroat.com

RIOT IN YOUR THROAT BOOKS

Sarah Beddow   *Dispatches from Frontier Schools*
Kathryn Bratt-Pfotenhauer   *Bad Animal*
Kimberly Casey   *Where the Water Begins*
Sonia Greenfield   *All Possible Histories*
Brett Elizabeth Jenkins   *Brilliant Little Body*
Melissa Fite Johnson   *Green*
Melissa Fite Johnson   *Midlife Abecedarian*
Hadley Jones   *Devout*
Hilary King   *Stitched on Me*
Frances Klein   *Another Life*
Courtney LeBlanc   *Exquisite Bloody, Beating Heart*
Courtney LeBlanc   *Her Dark Everything*
Shilo Niziolek   *Little Deaths*
Laura Passin   *Borrowing Your Body*
Sara Quinn Rivara   *Little Beast*
Laurie Rachkus Uttich   *Somewhere, a Woman Lowers the Hem of Her Skirt*
Karen J Weyant   *Avoiding the Rapture*